Investing

An Instructional Manual For Managing Rental Properties
Remotely And Achieving Financial Independence

*(How To Invest In Real Estate To Build Wealth Or A Stable
Stream Of Passive Income)*

Nathaniel Rowland

TABLE OF CONTENT

The Goal And Role Of The Stock Market

The global financial system is regulated by the stock market. Stock markets are used by businesses to make money, as well as by individual traders to buy and sell shares of stock. The regulation of stock exchange prices and practices is one of the main goals of stock markets. They control the exchange of financial assets as well. For businesses and investors, these restrictions facilitate a fair trading environment. The development of the economy requires such a setting.

A platform for trading shares of publicly traded corporations is provided by stock markets. The markets offer excellent chances for firms to generate money and so reflect the health of a nation's economy. The stock market's function is to:

Connect Buyers and Sellers

The stock market functions as a marketplace that connects buyers and sellers in an effort to facilitate transactions between those looking to buy shares and those looking to sell them. For instance, you would need to work with a broker to trade Microsoft shares on your behalf. You can also choose to speak with persons selling Microsoft shares directly in order to learn about prices and trading practices. Some contemporary markets automatically match buyers and sellers. The transaction procedure is streamlined because everything is completed immediately. Due to the real-time nature of these transactions, the market is highly efficient and there are few brokerage fees and commissions.

Verify Fair Trade

Each stock market is governed by rules and regulations. These are constantly implemented to guarantee that investors receive the greatest offers available. In order for this to happen, the stock exchange must supply investors with the data they need to make educated judgments. This information is freely available on the platforms and aids investors in choosing which transactions to enter into and what to anticipate from such transactions. It offers details including a stock's historical costs, how many shares have been sold thus far, and the current bid and ask prices.

Investors can decide whether to trade in particular equities based on this information.

Make Business Operations easier

The stock market is one way for businesses to raise money for growth. The same markets are used by organizations for both operational and strategic growth. This include facilitating mergers and acquisitions, setting up a business' entry into new markets, and creating new business infrastructure. A company's credibility may increase if it lists its shares on the stock market. This becomes crucial when negotiating contracts with prospective partners and clients since they can assess the company's legitimacy.

Some businesses pay their shareholders and employees through the stock market. To recruit and keep the finest workers in the business, programs like employee stock ownership, restricted stock, and other stock-based remuneration might be implemented.

Encourage Organizational Growth

The stock market can be used by businesses looking to grow to raise money to support this growth. These resources originate from public investors that support the company. By employing this method, the group can raise money without having to pound on the doors of banks and investors. To do this, the company clearly states the share prices and trading conditions and lists a portion of its shares on the stock market. The initial public offering, or IPO, that is taking place with this listing. The general public then acquires the IPO at predetermined pricing and pays the listing organization with the proceeds. The business then uses this cash to grow its operations. More goods and services translate into more resources for society.

Regulate Businesses

Platforms for stock exchange trading are crucial for managing business operations. A yearly financial report and balance sheet must be submitted to the trading platform by every company that registers its stock on the stock market. This makes sure that only trustworthy businesses continue to trade on the stock market and that no shady organizations can last more than a year. Companies who fail to provide the necessary paperwork frequently end themselves on blacklists and are unable to sell their shares on these platforms.

Financial Preparation

The focus of all financial planning operations is the stock market. The platforms give you the option of holding your equities in a more indirect manner through mutual funds or in your brokerage account. The ability to choose from a large variety of equities coming from various businesses and industries is provided by stock markets. Growth stocks are a type of stock that can be quite volatile but can also generate a sizable income for some investors. The majority of these are bought by aggressive investors who are unafraid of the risk associated with such purchases. More cautious investors exchange preferred stocks and other less volatile securities. Those who lack the time to thoroughly analyze individual firms may want to think about investing in mutual funds that simultaneously track several indices.

Maintain Economic Effectiveness

The stock market has a significant impact on economic systems because it distributes cash to firms, encouraging them to produce more goods for everyone's benefit. Market forces favor businesses that continue to increase their market share. Markets for stocks do not recognize companies that do poorly in the marketplace.

The majority of investors only buy stock from businesses that are profitable and have good capital management. In order to survive on the stock market, weak companies may think about merging with more successful ones. Such businesses will either continue to struggle in their operations or may completely vanish from the market if this does not take place.

the perceptions of the economy

The perception that investors have of particular markets plays a significant role in preserving their stability. For instance, nations like the United States and the United Kingdom have a great reputation for encouraging stock investments even when their economies are struggling.

Emerging markets are those nations where stock prices are constantly rising. Strong economies are those nations that are already well-established on the stock market. Such impressions have a significant impact on the economies of the countries. For instance, because emerging economies have such great potential for growth, the majority of local and foreign investors always look to invest in them.

However, when stock markets in developed economies see a decline in value, the repercussions could be very negative. For instance, after the US stock market crashed in 1929, the world's economy struggled for about 10 years until the great depression began. This suggests that a strong economy and stock markets do correlate with one another.

One of the most effective indicators of a nation's economy is how well it does on the stock market. A stronger economy draws more investors, which raises the nation's returns. Most of the time, index prices of the many stocks traded on the market by the nation can be used to foretell booms or depressions.

Investor protection

Most stock exchanges operate autonomously. To guarantee that strict regulations regulate stock trading and the stock market as a whole, they coordinate with regulatory organizations. Companies that trade on stock exchanges are subject to strict rules regarding corporate governance and ethical behavior. These regulations guarantee the safety of investors and other market participants from unethical and fraudulent events.

Financial Promotion

In one way or another, all investments, no matter how tiny, help the economy expand. The stock market continues to attract new investors every day as physical markets focus on enacting laws that are less advantageous to investors. The majority of these investors enter the market with the intention of purchasing shares from businesses with strong development prospects. By only dealing in shares, some of the most seasoned investors have amassed billions of dollars. The diversity of stocks that are accessible for investment on stock markets that draw foreign entities gives investors more choices.

Investors can purchase the listed stock once a firm issues an IPO. When the stock sells for more than it cost to buy it, a profit is realized. When they sell the stock for less than they paid when they got it, they suffer losses. This is the building block of stock trading. An investor's ability to spend and reinvest increases when they generate a profit. Less money is available for these activities when an investor loses money, which in turn lowers the amount of money in society.

Risk Management

In most stock market operations, there is some risk involved. Even the most stable equities occasionally experience dramatic price declines. Regulators on the stock market work to stop this kind of decline in stock values. Investors now have the chance to trade without being concerned about losing all of their money.

The regulators accomplish this by scrutinizing each company listed on the market and only permitting businesses with a significant amount of historical data to participate in stock trading. Any company that wants to continuously list its shares on the stock market must deliver financial statements at set intervals. Since they already hold confidential information about the company, the authorities also prevent insiders of these companies from purchasing and selling shares of the same company. The level of risk that investors encounter is decreased by these restrictions and numerous more. Additionally, they guarantee price stability on the market, balancing the entire stock trading process.

Supply of Capital

The stock market's ability to give businesses speedy access to capital is another essential role. The stock market provides a venue where one company can simultaneously engage millions of investors. These investors can easily buy shares from the company while concentrating on selling these shares for more money days, weeks, or even years from now. The goal of the stock market is to maintain a constant flow of capital for all businesses that are listed there. Once an investment opportunity presents itself, businesses can take advantage of it to quickly raise billions of dollars. With such enormous sums of money available, a company's product line can be expanded, creating more work opportunities for the general public. This lowers the number of jobless cases while also generating some tax income for the government.

Many organizations would turn to banks and other lending institutions for loans if there were no stock markets. These are frequently returned with high interest rates, which the investor could find bothersome. By offering a venue where companies can obtain capital by allowing the general public to purchase shares of the company, the stock market reduces this necessity. Due to the fact that they are free from the obligation of paying dividends to shareholders, businesses benefit greatly from this.

Governments can also make money through the stock market. State and federal governments may need money to finish particular projects. Some states will raise the required money for these initiatives by raising taxes. However, some governments choose to use stock exchanges to sell their bonds. These projects are launched with the funds earned from the sale of these bonds by investors. Once such initiatives are finished, they naturally raise living standards and give some residents jobs. This ultimately results in a stronger economy.

Control equity prices

The price of securities is determined by the stock market. Depending on the levels of supply and demand for these securities, this occurs automatically. Securities issued by corporations with significant market values typically cost more than those offered by unprofitable and declining companies.

Trading firms, financial institutions, and governments all value the process of valuing stocks. They gain a better appreciation of the worth and possibilities of their investment. Governments can use this information to decide the amount of tax to be imposed on these securities, while creditors can use it to assess the creditworthiness of people and entities.

Facilitate secure transactions

Only those individuals and companies are allowed to trade equities that are listed on these exchanges. Only companies that are listed as traders are allowed to transact on stock exchanges. Businesses are included to this list only when they meet specific requirements. Listed companies must still abide by certain rules. This ensures the highest level of security for every transaction done on any stock market. The market is constantly utilizing better trading strategies for the benefit of all participants.

Liquidity of Stocks Growing

The stock market acts as a ready market for buyers wishing to invest in company shares. It allows traders and investors the peace of mind that their money may be converted into stock and their shares into money fast and easily. This is what motivates investors to make quick investments in long-term projects. The market makes it simple for investors to identify profitable companies, and it also helps them avoid stocks from companies that carry a high potential for loss.

Uphold Diversity

At the stock market, traders and investors assemble in one place. As these people engage, more interesting trade opportunities arise. The market offers small, inconsequential firms the chance to draw in investors who might not have known about them otherwise. As more people enter the market, new opportunities, ideas, and strategies emerge. As a result, more investor needs are met, which raises the probability of mergers and acquisitions.

Stock and financial institution markets

Through banks and other financial institutions, you have the possibility of generating income from your money. Some of them aren't aware that putting your deposits in the stock market could result in significant financial gains for them. The remainder of these profits could then be set aside to pay your interest. The majority of countries rely on banks to keep their economies stable. As a result, by allowing local banks to invest there, the stock market can strengthen a country's economy. On these markets, there are several investment opportunities that banks can take advantage of. SIP and mutual funds are two examples of investments that offer better returns than traditional saving methods.

Market Trading and Common People

Changes in the stock market have an impact on both investors and non-investors. Pensions and retirement fees are always affected by changes in the stock market. This is due to the possibility that a person's decision to retire early could be impacted by weak market conditions.

When share prices fall, negative economic impacts are typically felt all around. The economy is impacted by even the smallest changes in price swings. The stock market and economy may not be very similar, but changes in one will always have an effect on the other. This is done so that the stock market's listed companies' worth can be appreciated. The prosperity of these companies is an indication of the state of the economy as a whole.

Consumer spending and market conditions

Basically, changes in the stock market always have an effect on consumer spending. During a bull market, consumers often spend more because they anticipate larger profit margins. When the market is bearish, consumers often spend less because there is a higher chance that they will lose their money.

When commodity prices rise, the consumer is more confident that the trade will be profitable. As a result, spending constraints are relaxed. Investors also have a propensity to spend more during this time since they expect to profit from the market. When this happens, businesses create more sales and consequently more revenue.

When the stock market falls, wealth erosion could happen. Customers regard this unfavorably and often make less purchases as a result. As a result, businesses suffer because their sales produce little or no profit.

For instance, consumer spending suffered greatly during the Great Depression of the 1930s. The graph below makes this very clear.

Figure 1.0 compares consumer expenditure with stock market performance.

Companies are impacted by the stock market's performance because it influences the value of their shares. Companies may need to raise more funds by selling shares at lower prices than planned when the stock market performs poorly.

The rewards are frequently higher when a company trades its shares in a steady stock market than they are when the market is struggling. This is due to the fact that when market performance is strong, more investors visit the market than when it is weak. During this time, businesses can also use the stock as a medium of exchange for growth. This occurs when a business buys out a faltering business and pays with highly valued stock rather than cash. As a result, the agreed-upon sum is paid in the form of shares that the owner of the struggling business can afterwards sell for a profit.

In general, alternative investment possibilities are impacted by changes in the stock market. For instance, when the stock market declines, investors become more interested in the bond market. Investors will look for new avenues of profit as the market declines, and at this point, they may examine securities like government bonds. These investments give higher returns at current moment. When consumers observe a decline in their wealth, it is one of the key signs that stock prices are declining. Even though stock market investors are frequently ready for losses, if they persist, they will typically start looking for alternate assets.

Market fluctuations frequently have indirect effects on things like pensions. The majority of pension plan providers always place a portion of their funds in the stock market. Such organizations might not be able to raise the funds necessary to pay retirees in a timely manner when stock values drop. This implies that certain payments will be made later or for less money than anticipated. Pension funds may suffer a lot if stock prices stay low for an extended length of time.

Non-investors may not notice short-term fluctuations in stock prices because the effects are seldom strong. Long-term changes, however, could affect the whole economy. The impact is always greatest on shareholders. Businesses might not be able to increase the required returns if the stock market decreases for an extended period of time. This implies that those shareholder distributions will be adversely impacted.

What Taxes Apply to Stocks?

You should be aware of how much in taxes you will have to pay as you try to learn more about how the stock market operates. In order to avoid having less money than you expected after a trade, it is necessary to keep tax rates in mind. In essence, there are two tax regimes for the stock market. The first is a qualified retirement account, and the second is an ordinary account. The majority of investors always hold shares in both sectors.

You have the ability to grow your money tax-free with qualified retirement accounts. You are subject to taxation when you withdraw money. You can invest your money and pay your taxes later thanks to them. This drastically lowers your tax obligation. You will be obliged to pay tax on both the amount you invested and the profits made from the investment when you withdraw the money. Investors frequently use these funds in anticipation of lower tax rates in retirement. Before investing your money in this sort of account, it is advised that you speak with your investment advisor because it has specific limits.

Taxes on unqualified investment accounts are usually double-taxed. Dividend income is subject to income tax, as are stock profit distributions. Companies are obligated to pay a tax, often 15%, on any dividends they give to shareholders. If you own a stock for more than a year, as an investor, the investment's gains will be taxed at long-term capital rates. Although there are a number of reasons why it might alter, this is always 15%. You must pay regular income tax on the gains made if you own a particular stock for less than a year. Depending on the tax bracket of the investor, this can be greater than 15%. Your tax or financial counselor can provide you with this information. Capital gain tax is the term used to describe the tax levied on stock investment earnings.

If you sell your shares at a loss, you can offset any capital gains with those losses.

This could significantly lower your tax obligations. You must be able to balance your trades as a stock trader to reduce the tax that is levied. For instance, it is wise to invest larger sums of money if you are trading using a qualified retirement account because doing so will result in lower taxes.

Knowledge of Capital Gains Tax

Any profit you make from selling stock when you invest in stock shares will inevitably be subject to taxation. Although the standard long-term capital gains tax is usually 15%, if you are in a lower tax category, you might only be subject to 5% of that amount.

Dividends are not taxed as capital gains but rather as normal income. Since the tax rate for dividends received through a qualifying account is between 0% and 15%, they are always favorable. Qualified dividends are those that are paid by a corporation with a stock holding period of more than 60 days, whether it is based in the United States or elsewhere. Before you begin, your broker can always offer you advice on this. Dividends from stocks held in eligible retirement accounts are not subject to taxation upon receipt. Normal tax rates apply to non-qualified dividends received from standard accounts. These consist of dividends from savings accounts, stock options, and other similar payments.

It's critical that you comprehend the inputs utilized in these computations when determining the returns you obtained from selling a stock. Changing a few parameters in the formula can help you pay less in taxes. Even while the majority of investors think they should be taxed on their whole profit, this shouldn't always be the case. Sales Proceeds - Capital (Basis) = Taxable

Income or Profit is the formula used to determine taxable income.

You can easily take transactional expenses like brokerage commissions out of the total amount of cash. The basis represents the price of the stock plus any dividends you may have reinvest in the stock market. The commissions that were paid to buy the current shares are also shown. If you are selling stock that you inherited from someone else, the basis will be determined by the stock's value on the date the deceased passed away. In the event that the stock is a gift, its price will reflect its market value at the time of the giving.

By selling stocks at a loss and then buying them back at almost the same price, some investors may avoid paying taxes. The wash rule, often known as the wash principle, enables this. However, if you buy the stock back within 30 days of selling it, some accounts won't let you record a loss.

The Losses Tax

The fact that you may only write off a certain amount of losses from your investments in stocks when filing your taxes is a major drawback. The standard amount you can deduct from your taxes annually if your stock sells at a loss is merely $3000. The remaining balance will be carried over to the following year if the losses incurred are more than this sum. The upside to this is that you can use losses to offset gains when filing your taxes.

Most investors fail to include in broker and advisory commissions when calculating their taxes. It's crucial to determine how much commission your broker has been deducting from your account so that you can factor that into your calculations. The IRS may send you a letter informing you that you owe money in taxes if you sell a stock but fail to include the capital gain tax in your other tax payments. Most investors aim to balance gains with losses in order to keep their tax obligations to a minimal.

The Benefits Of Investing In Dividend Stocks

The stock market allows for the deployment of a wide variety of tactics. Some people merely want to profit from the shares' price growth. Share prices of stocks often increase over the long term. As a result, you can amass a sizable portfolio of shares, and when you're ready to retire, you can start selling them off piecemeal for cash gains. You can then live off the money. This type of investor is likely not going to be interested in dividend stocks.

Others attempt to make quick money. Traders are people who buy and sell stocks with the intention of making quick money. A trader is a person who purchases stock at a price that is thought to be low, waits for the price to increase to a level where profits are acceptable, and then sells their shares. Of fact, we are only describing the ideal scenario because it is much more difficult than it seems to trade equities for a profit. Instead of making money, most day traders lose money.

Investors who receive dividends prefer to keep their stocks. A dividend investor makes an investment with the intention of profiting from the cash dividends that the stock offers. Therefore, these assets generate revenue. As a dividend investor, the only genuine situation in which you might think about offloading stock is if the business starts to perform poorly or worse. You could keep holding the stock indefinitely if a company keeps its market share and performance. Your objective is to be able to use dividend payments to supplement or possibly cover all of your living expenditures.

We'll go into more detail about the rationale behind dividend investing in this chapter. Compound interest will be used to demonstrate how reinvesting your profits into increasing investments can cause them to skyrocket in value. The common practice among dividend investors is to reinvest dividend payments while you are still employed and able to collect income from other sources in order to maximize the growth of your investment. This will entail expanding it by regularly buying fresh shares of stock as well as reinvested dividends to acquire additional shares of stock. In this way, your investments are growing dramatically with each passing quarter, laying the groundwork for a strong, steady income when you decide to stop growing your investments and retire. You will then be able to subsist on your dividend income as well as any additional income you may have, such as social security.

Income from retirement, and am I too old?

But consider the financial freedom. Nowadays, a little 401(k) plan is relied upon by so many people that they may not even pay attention to or comprehend it. They also anticipate receiving funds from social security benefits. In contrast, you could accumulate a strong portfolio of dividend-paying companies that will provide you with sizable payouts when you retire in 10, twenty, or thirty years.

No of your age, you ought to think about purchasing dividend stocks. Naturally, the older you get, the more forceful you'll need to be to pull it off. No of your age, you may always use dividend stocks to generate some income. If you are physically fit and anticipate being able to work into your fifties or even early sixties, you can invest actively and amass a healthy portfolio that you can utilize to help with your living expenses in retirement. You probably won't be able to totally rely on a dividend stock portfolio if you are 50 or older. Older investors who are falling behind and must start increasing their investments will therefore need to be quite aggressive. This will include investing a sizeable portion of your available funds in stocks that don't pay dividends but are very likely to increase in value. Then, after the principal has increased, you can either cash out these stocks and use the money to support yourself or reinvest it into dividend-paying equities so that you can start receiving income then. But the fact remains that, given the amount of wealth required, it is unlikely that you will ever be able to live off of simply investing in slow-growing equities.

A lot of financial gurus advocate arranging a portfolio of investments in percentages. You must seek the advice of a personal financial advisor or exercise your own discretion while creating your portfolio because this book does not provide investment advice. But if you're 50 or older, you might want to think about investing between 67% and 80% of your income in high-growth firms that don't pay dividends and 30% to 35% in dividend-paying stocks. As you get closer to the point where you're thinking about retiring, you can start shifting your portfolio more toward dividend-paying equities if you're disciplined and capable of maintaining your investment plan.

If you intend to hold stocks in which you want to increase your wealth only through share price growth, the typical guideline is to sell around 4% of your portfolio each year in order to generate cash. This is merely a suggestion, though, and we are unable to offer guidance because we are unaware of the precise circumstances of any readers, and these circumstances will vary from investor to investment. To ensure that you receive the quarterly income from the stocks, one option is to start selling off your equities once they have increased in value and then to start buying more shares of dividend-paying stocks. In this manner, you can start making money while maintaining a full investment.

Younger people have a longer time horizon to gradually increase their dividend portfolio. If you are under 45, you may afford to be more cautious and concentrate on a strategy for gradually building up a sizable dividend portfolio.

Additive Interest

Although the idea of compound interest is frequently covered in algebra classrooms, by the time people reach adulthood, the majority of them have forgotten about it. The power of saving and investing is demonstrated through compound interest. When interest is gained on money and reinvested, the investment "compounds" with each period of interest. This ultimately means that the investment will increase exponentially if you continue to make regular contributions to it. This straightforward idea formerly meant that if you deposited money in the bank, thirty years later you would have a million dollars. Banks are no longer worth utilizing other than to store some cash away for emergencies because they no longer pay very much. But thankfully for us, dividend stocks can fill this function.

Actually, dividend stocks perform better. The principal that you invest—the initial sum of money that you put into the account—actually decreases in value when you deposit money into a bank account or a certificate of deposit (CD). This is due to inflation, the perpetual and largely imperceptible tax that reduces the purchasing power of money every year. Although inflation has been modest in recent years, it is nevertheless present and depletes your principal. You need an interest rate that first takes into account the rate of inflation and then increases on top of that if you want to turn a profit. It must be at least 2-3% in order to take inflation into consideration.

According to a search for Ally Bank CD interest rates, they range from 2.3% to 2.6% (note that these figures are subject to change at any time and are only valid at the time of writing). If inflation is about 2%, investing in these kinds of financial securities will earn you essentially nothing. It is, at best, a means of saving some money for security.

A stock like IBM, meanwhile, provides a yield of nearly 4%.

However, dividend stocks do more than just pay "interest". A stock's initial investment often increases with time. So, for instance, IBM was about $25 per share in 1995. At the moment, each share is trading for $140. Not all stocks will increase in value in this manner, but if you have been investing in IBM, the value of your initial investment has increased significantly as a result of the stock's rising share price, and you are also receiving dividend payments, which serve the same purpose as interest in a savings account or bank certificate of deposit. Therefore, rather than only having compound interest, dividend stocks also have compounding compound interest.

Let's now think about how compound interest can help you expand your money. In the scenario that follows, it is assumed that you start with $1,000 and add $500 per month to your investments. With a 4% interest rate over 10 years, you would have $75,000 at the conclusion of the time frame.

With a $10,000 initial investment and $500 a month at 4% interest, after 20 years, you would have $204,428.

We need to take into account both the stock appreciation and the interest payment in order to determine how dividend stocks would increase in value. This may lead to an effective interest rate of 7% or even higher. Although the S & P 500's value increases by about 7% annually, we are not required to utilize such a high figure. Let's assume that the shares' total yearly growth and dividend yield came to 8%. We will now take a second look at that same 20-year investment with an additional $500 monthly payment. At the end of the 20 years, only that move would increase your account balance by more than $100,000.

This is significant because many dividend-paying stocks will increase their payouts above this level in order to retain the yield, and many will increase it even further. Accordingly, the value of your portfolio as measured by the value of your shares will be just as significant as the dividend yield (interest rate).

It is important to increase the amount you invest each month. If you invested $1,000 each month to purchase additional shares rather than $500, and your total interest rate, including appreciation and dividend yield, was 8% over the course of 20 years, your account would be valued more than $600,000.

You would have an account worth more than $200,000 even after ten years. That suggests that older investors can also gain from taking a risky approach.

Financial independence and passive income

Of course, the sooner you begin, the better, but it is clear that dividend stocks are advantageous. You will receive passive income from them. Once you have amassed enough shares to be content with the size of your portfolio, you will begin to receive consistent and dependable dividend payments in the form of cash each quarter. This could be incorporated into your passive income plan. If a person is able to amass enough shares to earn an income at or above the middle class level, they may be able to generate all of their income from dividend stocks. Anything above that, such as social security benefits, will be a bonus rather than a necessity for you to make ends meet.

To earn the amount of money they desire each year, many investors will need to combine dividend equities with stocks with fast growth. But regardless of the route you choose, you will be financially independent once you can make $50,000 or more a year from stock investments. At that time, you no longer rely on a job, a boss, or the government for your income. You are not compelled to work in order to exist, but you are free to choose to do so. Being able to live joyfully and economically without relying on others for your money is what financial independence is all about.

What must I invest, and how much?

It will be crucial to have a broad notion of the number of shares you must purchase to achieve various amounts of dividend income. Naturally, the situation is dynamic, meaning that it is constantly changing, so we cannot rely on a hasty guess today to tell what we will actually need in ten or twenty years. However, the projections will be reasonably correct.

Allow US to begin with $20,000. While we will later urge clients to create a fully diversified portfolio, for the purposes of this section's exercises we will take a single stock as an example. Take Abbvie, a pharmaceutical company, for example. There are good reasons why it is a highly well-liked investment. First of all, Abbvie has been around for more than a century. Second, over a 46-year period, dividend payments have increased. The yield is 6.53%, which is significantly greater than the interest rates that are currently offered by banks. The share's annual dividend is $4.28. The company is strong in terms of paying dividends, as seen by the payout ratio of 54.5%, and it has plenty of space to expand.

Shares are currently trading for $65 each. Of course, the amount may change significantly in ten years, but how much would you have to put up now if you wanted a $20,000 income?

Considering a $4.28 dividend per share, this calls for

$20,0/$4.28 equals 4,673 shares.

Cost of this:

4,673 x $65 = $303,745

I hope the readers are not shocked by this amount. It is a reasonable estimate, and unless you choose outliers, the amount you must invest will depend on yield and remain largely constant regardless of the stocks you choose.

We can deduce from this estimate that we must invest $759,000 in order to earn $50,000 year from this investment. This example demonstrates that you must gradually build up a dividend portfolio for income reasons if you don't already have a sizable quantity of funds available. There has never been a better moment to start investing in dividend-paying companies than right now, if you don't already have any.

You would need to purchase 23,365 shares of Abbvie in order to earn $100,000 annually. It would set you back $1.5 million.

Some stocks have substantially greater payments each year. For instance, Creditor LTD (BAC) pays $20 in dividends per share. The stock is $205 in price. You would need to purchase 1,000 shares of this stock in order to earn $20,000 annually. The price would be $205,000. Although it costs almost a third less than Abbvie, the payout ratio of 126% is unhealthily high. Therefore, it would be necessary to conduct some research in order to decide whether or not that stock is worthwhile. You run the danger of those high $20 dividends per share declining dramatically in the future, even if it's possible that the company will be able to maintain dividend payments given its projected future growth. A safer investment is Abbvie.

Drips And Dividend Reinvestment Plans

If you already have a sizable sum of money to invest, the information in this part won't apply to you. In that situation, you can purchase the necessary number of shares to achieve your chosen level of income and begin taking advantage of your dividend income.

Your dividend investment plan will require two distinct periods, though, if you are just starting out. You will use the first phase to increase the number of shares you currently possess. This period of time can run for years or even decades, depending on how aggressively you buy stocks and how much you can invest each month. We are presuming that you have another source of income that you can utilize to live on for the time being while investing throughout this period as you won't be interested in taking money out for income. This implies that you ought to make an effort to acquire as many shares as you can. One strategy for doing this is to reinvest all dividend income you get into more stock purchases. This process should be carried out up until the second and final stage of your dividend investing plan, when you can unwind and start receiving the quarterly dividend payments to use as income.

An investment plan for dividends therefore typically has two phases: the investing phase and the income phase.

You can either set up things such that it is done on your behalf throughout the investment phase, or you can rely on your own discipline to reinvest money. You ought to sign up for a DRIP, or dividend reinvestment plan, if you are able to do so. Your dividends are automatically used to purchase more shares when you sign up for DRIPs. Therefore, if you own shares of Chevron, the money from dividend payments will be used to purchase additional Chevron shares rather than providing you cash. These kinds of schemes allow you to purchase fractional shares in addition to enforcing discipline by ensuring that the money is actually being used to purchase more shares. Although it may not sound tempting, buying fractional shares over time will result in actual dividend income. especially if you plan to invest over a ten-year or longer time frame.

As a result, if you invested in IBM at $140 per share and received $70 in dividend income during a particular quarter, a DRIP would enable you to buy 1/2 of an additional share instead of pocketing the $70. That would be four additional shares of IBM stock over the course of a year, in addition to those that you may have purchased independently as part of your ongoing investing strategy.

And the larger your share purchases made via DRIPs are doing to become, the more shares you own over time.

Why Planning Is Important

One issue that new self-directed investors have is that they begin purchasing stocks without having a solid investment strategy. One of the worst things you can do is that. Setting goals and creating a plan to achieve them are both necessary. Remember that the strategy doesn't have to be etched in stone. You can modify the plan as needed as things develop. Ideally, as time passes, you will have more money to invest and will be able to buy more stocks on a regular basis, expanding your portfolio.

Doing your dividend analysis (Chapter 1), your fundamental analysis (Chapter 8), and establishing a strategy for successful investing (Chapter 4) are the first three components of an investment plan. You can choose equities to invest in from here.

Choosing how many shares of stock you will buy on a recurring basis is the second component of your plan. The ability to develop and follow such a strategy with discipline can frequently be the difference between success and failure.

Setting ambitious goals at first is not necessary. When first starting off, you should focus on creating habits. Therefore, it is not important how many shares of stock you buy each week; what matters is that you start buying one share each week and make it a habit. In the future, you can begin purchasing two shares per week, then three shares, and so forth. Avoid considering that you must complete everything all at once. Of course, you don't want to be so cautious that it hurts your investments, but you will eventually need to be more bold if you want to buy enough stock to generate enough dividend income to support yourself. But since you have to start somewhere, it is advisable to begin with a stock in the middle of the price range (maybe $50 to $80 per share) and to purchase one share at a time until you are ready to increase your investment.

People who are eager to start can make blunders and waste a lot of money at once. It is advised that you begin your investment profession carefully and deliberately in order to establish a strong procedure, even if you are a late starter. You don't have to invest every last cent right away; instead, you want to establish a reliable behavior habit that is long-lasting.

Effects of a Dividend Lifestyle on Taxes

Dividends are often not taxed at the capital gains rate. To determine whether the dividend payments you are receiving are qualified or not, you must first make an assessment.

Qualifying dividend income is taxed as capital gains. The average person's capital gains tax rate is between 15% and 20%, depending on their overall income. You can pay the capital gains tax rate, which is not only more manageable but also lower, on the majority of dividends you get from American businesses since they are considered eligible dividends.

There are particular holding requirements. You must have possessed the stock for at least 60 days prior to the ex-dividend date to qualify for the capital gains tax treatment. Some of those investments do, however, provide additional tax advantages. Unqualified dividends include those obtained from business development firms, master limited partnerships, or real estate investment trusts (REITS).

If you owned a stock for fewer than 60 days prior to the ex-dividend date, the payout would be regarded as unqualified for taxable purposes, at least for that quarter. This suggests that you will be required to pay ordinary income taxes on any dividend income you receive under those conditions.

Most dividend investors won't be worried about these tax issues. This is due to the fact that before you start collecting income from your investment, you will have owned it for a while, in which case all of your dividends will be qualifying dividends.

According to Chapter 5, are ETFs really the best investment option?

High average growth rates are consistently produced by Western stock markets. Equity indices in other Western countries and the S&P 500 index, which gauges the value of the 500 best-performing listed American firms, have climbed by an average of 10% during the past century.

You don't need an MBA to grasp why yields are so high—significantly higher than real estate yields. For instance, Nestle is a major producer of foods, Motorola is a manufacturer of communications equipment that you've undoubtedly used at least once in your life, and Microsoft creates technology items such as computer hardware and software. The only thing you'll receive from the apartment complex you wish to acquire, on the other hand, is heartburn from regular upkeep and supervision. Alternately, you might invest in a handful of the best publicly traded companies, sit back, and watch your building's superintendent fix your leaky faucet.

Most persons who engage in active investment management are not ideal candidates. There is never a reason to believe that you can "beat the market" and generate an average return that is higher than that of the equity indices. Academic studies questioned the worth of investment managers as early as the 1990s. According to a number of studies, including William Sharp's "The Arithmetic of Active Management," 98% of professional fund managers fail to provide their customers with an excess return that is larger than the market return.

How is it possible that a manager with in-depth knowledge, expertise, and analytical tools can not consistently produce an excess return for his clients?

He competes with other investment managers who have the same expertise, experience, and research, which is the straightforward answer.

Investment managers spend a lot of money on salaries, office space, and marketing due to this healthy rivalry. The average market return often stays the same even though investment managers occasionally outperform their rivals. Most managed funds turn a profit while the market is up, but the reverse is true during recessionary times.

A study of stock performance from 1926 to 2018 was carried out by University of Arizona economist Hendrik Bessembinder. He discovered that starting in 1926, the growth of the entire market can be attributed to just 4% of the shares that are traded on the stock exchange at any given moment. Let me explain what this implies before you put this book away for the day. You shouldn't have made the investment if it depended on 96% of the companies trading on the stock exchange.

Professional investment managers are searching for those fantastic 4% stocks that, in a specific year, would soar stock market indices to new heights.

The bad news is that nobody can forecast the future, not even the finest investment managers. They might be aware of a few stocks that will help the index, but it's improbable that they could pinpoint the precise 4% that will produce the majority of the gain each year. Because of this, 98% of investment managers have failed to produce returns that are higher than those of the top stock indices for several years.

There is, however, some good news. Because they incorporate the entire market, ETFs that follow leading stock indices are made up of the top 4% of performers. You don't need to search for the newest, hottest companies when you purchase an ETF because you already have them on your list!

Of course, there are times when an investor's nightmare is the stock market.

The foolish propensity of an investor to fall in love with investing holdings is one of the psychological flaws that humans have to deal with. Investors frequently become emotionally invested in a stock when its value increases. The same inclination makes novice investors loathe equities that result in losses. So they sell them in the heat of the moment, at a low price, which is actually the worst possible time to sell.

Family, friends, food, romance, home decor, and other things can all benefit from emotions, but not your stock portfolio. Equity index investing is a sensible strategy to take emotions out of the financial portfolio. because you're not falling in love with one dynamite company with potential — you're investing in an entire market with hundreds or even thousands of companies represented.

The uncomfortable truth is that most active investors believe they are superior to all other investors due to the illusion of control. Jealousy, anxiety, exhilaration, and other psychological problems are all stuffed into every human being. There's nothing wrong with it, but each of these feelings could be another inner voice that prevents your account's interest from accruing.

If I had the ability to bio-hack the ideal long-term investor, I would render it blind, deaf, and unable to ever connect to a Wi-Fi network. a kind of dispassionate cyborg that makes investments, deposits, and savings decisions on its own. Unfortunately, this is an unreasonable expectation of anyone who is deemed to be human, therefore the best one can hope for from good investors is that they will admit their flaws, practice yoga, do some breathing exercises, call a buddy, have a snack, and try to act as rationally as they can.

Israeli behavioral psychology professors Daniel Kahneman and Amos Tversky's research indicates that fear of loss influences our decisions more than pleasure from gain. Most people tend to avoid dangers because of a "bug" in our system. This explains the biggest mistake made by the average investor: rather than buying a variety of stocks, waiting decades, and enjoying rising returns, the average investor will buy stocks based on gut instinct or news headlines, then get scared and withdraw their money at the first sign of market volatility.

Let's be lazy investors and discuss a multi-stage investment strategy in the capital market rather than being average investors:

Invest in an ETF that tracks a large index.

Sit on it for a long time. Never panic when there is a small increase, and never panic sell when there is a small decline. Don't even download a stock app to check your portfolio on your phone. Just let it be. Let it operate. Investors, be sluggish!

The ideal investment is an ETF that tracks an index. Unless they are?

ETFs aren't the ideal investment tools. This is due to the fact that there isn't a perfect investment product. They do, however, provide investors with a straightforward execution strategy and enable investors to quickly and easily amass income-producing assets. You can only guarantee that your investments will work if you follow this multi-stage approach without interfering and over an extended period of time.

Sounds Simple!

The lazy investment strategy does appear simple to execute. It simply requires purchasing and holding, after all. No ambiguity there. It is possible to fall for financial gurus, self-interested investment managers, and media manipulation. They all share the following two traits:

They wish to keep you in the dark and afraid.

They demand your cash.

After starting your "buy and hold" "lazy investor" method, you must make a commitment never to sell without careful consideration. In times of loss, you can enter the bathroom, shut the door, face the mirror, and recite aloud to yourself that you haven't lost anything if you haven't sold. Additionally, if you haven't gained at this point, you definitely haven't held for long enough.

Your investing account may experience extended periods of red numbers (a loss), maybe years. Simply turning off the computer and pursuing another hobby will help you get through those times.

Many of my friends asked me how much of their stock portfolio they should sell during the March 2020 global financial crisis. New investors were horrified to see their hard-earned money disappear. Investors who began their investments two years before to the crisis saw all of their gains go in a single month. I gave a clear and direct response: Don't sell anything! I also reassured them that if they made market investments like a responsible investor would, a global epidemic shouldn't be a cause for fear in the long run. I repeatedly emphasized to my friends that the economy had already weathered numerous pandemics, world wars, and natural calamities, and that it would also survive COVID-19. In hindsight, it appears that the economy expanded!

The most lazy and passive investor portfolios quickly recovered to their prior high-value performance, just four months after the market crashed. Additionally, during the crisis, those who continued to follow this hands-off investment strategy and added to their monthly share purchases made money! This only serves to demonstrate that the lazy approach should not be modified, even during economic hardship:

Order Hold

The lazy investor has another superpower in addition to this "buy and hold" approach and apathetic endurance to market fluctuations: investment diversification.

We are frequently only given the ability to choose between a few options in many facets of life. With investing, that is not the case. You can go down that route on your own, sure, but investing diversification is like that free banquet you only occasionally get. So why not benefit from it? This is a tried-and-true method for decreasing volatility and disaster-proofing your investment portfolio in the world of investments. The nicest part is that you don't have to make any sacrifices in order to have that choice.

It's true that financial guru blogs and newspaper headlines frequently scream about soaring stocks because that's what sells or draws attention. The issue is that traditional businesses that generate reliable, consistent revenue and have expanded over many years make up the great bulk of the market rather than unicorn start-ups that go public and sell for billions. These businesses do not generate ratings, hence they are not the newsmakers. Rarely will you find articles about Kevin or Janet's fulfilling Monday through Friday, 9 to 5 positions in middle management. Those are not compelling reading. However, someone would write about Sandy, a small-town assembly-line worker, if she won the state lottery's multi-million dollar jackpot. She would travel to Disneyland and everyone would know!

It is a waste of time, effort, and money to try to "beat the market" by making investments in what you believe to be your investment lottery winner. The trading platforms (which charge the hunter-investor commissions for each transaction performed) and the government tax collectors (who charge for every profit, even unintentional profits, by collecting the requisite tax), are the two parties who always profit when the investor is involved in the same hunt. Like you, the lazy investor simply lets his money grow, pays the investing firm a minimal commission, and postpones paying taxes until he or she decides to do so. For instance, I came to the conclusion that since I expect to invest forever, the only time I would have to pay taxes on my investment income was when the world ended.

Are there any drawbacks to ETFs?

ETFs could come as a bit of a cultural shock and may insult your sensibilities as a person of detail if you're the kind of person who wants to thoroughly grasp what you're investing in. To become a lazy investor, though, you must first ask yourself why you would want to do so in the first place.

You can get rid of the need to micromanage your investment portfolio by just realizing, accepting, and knowing that your account won't make you a millionaire over night.

Write the phrase "A GOOD INVESTMENT IS A BORING INVESTMENT" on a blank sheet if you need encouragement with your new perspective. Now print this page and stick it to a wall where you can view it every morning when you wake up. Repeat the phrase several times in your thoughts each time you visit that page. then carry on with your regular day. Thank you very much.

How Do ETFs That Follow Popular Trends Fare?

It is real. They are real. However, they are referred to as a "trend" for a reason.

For a brief period, it is seen as hot or popular. Trendy ETFs do not fit the lax investment approach. How many of you are hurriedly making purchases of Pet Rocks? How many of you are truly familiar with those?

Perhaps you currently believe that a cannabis ETF is the way to go, but is that the best addition to your portfolio for lazy investors? It's money bloggers and YouTubers who make those investments seem cool or seductive. However, as passive investors, we seek long-term, optimal growth. But I can tell you that investment firms adore fashionable ETFs! Why? because of the enormous management fees! Some of them even reach 1%! (Believe me. When you total it up, it's a lot.) Trendy investments are the "shiny balls" of the financial world, and you don't have to be an expert in marketing to appreciate this. However, for you, the sluggish investor, they are hardly investment magic.

How Do Etfs Function?

In actuality, there isn't much to comprehend. An organization creates the ETF, buys shares in direct proportion to the size of the index firms, and deposits those shares with a trustee. How is it that an ETF can be less expensive per unit when a single share of the corporation would be more expensive? For instance, one share of the Vanguard Total World Stock ETF (VT) costs roughly US$104. However, if purchased separately from VT, Amazon (stock symbol: AMZN), one of the assets, would cost about US$3,300.

Let's use another instance to illustrate this. A S&P 500 ETF today represents the top American corporations if you choose to purchase it. In other words, you instantly acquire a little stake in 500 well-known and prosperous businesses, including Facebook, McDonald's, Wal-Mart, and Disney.

An ETF that tracks an index need not follow stock market indexes. There are indices that monitor the performance of bonds as well as indexes that represent the cost of commodities like corn and oil. But let's stop there for the time being because the book isn't meant to make you into corn tycoons.

ETFs have the significant advantage of reducing the issuer's risk.

ETFs offer a variety of investment choices, just like other products like mutual funds and ETNs (Exchange Traded Notes). Mutual fund stocks legally and contractually belong to investors; in fact, they are held in trust by a different bank than the investment firm that produces them, which is the distinction that makes ETFs superior to the other products. This gives lazy investors like you and me a lot of confidence and reduces investor risk in scenarios like if your investment house—the individuals in charge of managing your portfolio—suddenly, for any reason, went out of business.

It works like this: If you give a friend a loan of money, the money is kept securely in a bank and can only be accessed with both of your signatures. You may be sure that your friend cannot obtain the money without your signature if he decides to depart town or develops a blackjack addiction. You can also reconsider your friendship.

Are ETFs a quick way to invest?

In no way. In investing, there are no short cuts. When you purchase an index-tracking ETF, the various investment firms that issue the ETFs are actually providing a service for which you pay a management charge (also known as an expense ratio). Due to the often modest administration fees, this isn't actually a drawback. These management fees are actually among the lowest in the financial markets when it comes to ETFs. In comparison to the fees paid to active managers who manage your mutual funds, various retirement plans, or managed investment portfolios, they're unquestionably lot less expensive.

A dollar paid to an investment house is a dollar lost, therefore management fees are a zero-sum game. However, every dollar you save will continue to benefit you in the future.

The result is clear: when you invest in passive funds rather than active funds, you pay more for the stocks in your investment portfolio and less for wages, offices, and computers (i.e., operating expenses of investing firms). Index-tracking ETFs charge incredibly low management fees in a time when investment managers are not ashamed to demand exorbitant sums on investment portfolios in the neighborhood of 1% of the investment portfolio. Because the issuing company does not conduct in-depth analysis on indices, there are cost variations. They exist only to, uh, track the index.

Let's examine this utilizing the following example:

"Dollar" Belle is in charge of the Big Money Investment House's fund. With a securities license, a bachelor's in business administration, a master's in economics, and other credentials, Belle has long been a top performer for her clients. She has undoubtedly earned her moniker, in addition to a corner office, a sports car, and a respectable $140,000 income.

Dollar Belle's office is directly across the street from the Vanguard trading room, where a large number of interns and junior employees spend each day checking that the passive fund tracking the S&P 500 index includes the 500 largest public companies traded on the US stock market in proportion to their weight in the index, among other things.

Due to this distinction, the managed fund of Dollar Belle would charge the investor an excessive management fee of 0.8% while the passive fund will be content with less than a tenth of that (0.07%). While Vanguard's ETF uses far less (it just tracks the index) on behalf of millions of investors, Dollar Belle's office spends quite a bit of time and money on a relatively small number of investors.

Do the variations in the management charge make sense as petty cash? Check out this illustration of a $100,000 investment portfolio:

In the first year of investing with a manager like Dollar Belle, a 0.8% management fee costs the investor (the client) $800.

A passive investment portfolio owner who only uses index funds will pay a minimal 0.07% management charge, which will cost them about $70 in the first year.

This results in a net save of $730 each year. There will always be those who choose to shell out cash for the skills and experience of a gifted investment manager like Dollar Belle. You must pay for quality service, thus that is very legitimate. But don't you think it would be better if you knew exactly how much you were spending and what you were getting in return?

We already read in the book how, over a number of decades, the average market return will nearly always be greater than the return Dollar Belle will experience. However, if we only consider the management fee portion, we'll see that the small percentages that are eating away at your investment portfolio mount up to extremely significant sums.

Let's assume for the purposes of illustration that the two portfolios we previously discussed provide an average return of 9% annually over a period of twenty years:

There is little doubt that Dollar Belle's active portfolio will expand significantly. The portfolio's worth is $483,666 in its 20th year. This includes deducting a total management charge of more than $40,000. (The findings given are approximate; actual results may vary slightly depending on the calculation's compounding frequency.)

After subtracting less than $4,000 in management costs, the passive portfolio, which merely tracks indexes and is not managed at all, will have a value of $553,286.

Warren Buffett's Investment Principles

We frequently make investing more difficult than necessary. Warren Buffet adopts a straightforward strategy founded in logic. By following Warren Buffett's investment advice, you will manage your portfolios more effectively, make fewer expensive mistakes, and get closer to your goals every day. Warren Buffett's investment guidance is timeless, and practically all of it can be summed up in the list of rules for investing that he provided below.

Avoid going bankrupt.

During the 2008 financial crisis, Buffett personally lost over $24 billion, and his business, Berkshire Hathaway, lost its esteemed AAA rating. How then can he counsel against financial loss? He's talking about an investor's perspective, I suppose. Don't waste anything. Avoid gambling. Don't approach an investment with the mindset that "losing is okay." Know the facts. Do your research. This guideline initially appears to go against some of his other investment advise, which states that one shouldn't invest in the stock market unless they can watch their stock holdings decrease by 50% without panicking. Once you realize that there is a distinction between losing money and observing a drop in the value of your portfolio, however, we can resolve this conflict. Without a sure, you will lose money if you panic-sell when the stock market has dropped by 50%, especially on your most recent purchases.

Nevertheless, if you stick it out through market downturns (often purchasing more shares when prices are low), you will ultimately come out ahead, all other things being equal. Therefore, when Buffett says "Never lose money," he only refers to crystallized financial losses and not to brief dips in paper cash. The underlying query is: How, given that he has recorded some substantial cash losses, Tesco being a famous example, can Buffett claim to "Never Lose Money"? The solution is in Buffett's method of investing. The majority of investors focus on potential gains when searching for possibilities, believing that a share "could rise to his previous glory years," "could rise to xx amount," or "I could double my money through this share within the next year," etc. Buffett adopts a different strategy; he begins by speculating on potential problems.

Is it possible for the company to suffer a catastrophic failure and a lasting capital loss? He isn't interested in a prospective upside; instead, he wants to know why a company might succeed. When deciding whether to invest in a firm, very few investors review the "principal risks and uncertainties" section of the balance sheet and cash flow statement of the annual report. According to Buffett's investing philosophy, we should conduct this research before being tempted by strong earnings growth, a big market opportunity, or high dividend yields.

This Buffett guideline simply implies investing in well-capitalized, high-margin companies that generate cash rather than adopting a casino mentality of "punt," "play money," and "risky bet."

Buffett avoids danger in another way, which is evident in the way he feels about debt. Given his cautious character, it is not unexpected that he is not a huge supporter of debt due to the risk that excessive debt can bring, whether we are discussing personal debt or debt that Berkshire or other firms have on their books. The issue with debt is that it might be terrible to use it excessively during difficult times. For instance, buying stocks on margin (that is, using borrowed funds from your broker) might be problematic when equities decline since your anxious broker will want its money back. Consider your credit card debt; the idea is the same. When things are good, you may use your credit card responsibly, pay your bills on time, and use the credit as it was intended to be used—as a tool, not a crutch.

However, if you over-relied on credit and racked up an unmanageable amount of debt by purchasing faux-mink neck warmers, gold coffee tables, and a felt of hot-air balloons, it's simple to fall behind after one lost job or significant unforeseen medical expenditure. Despite the fact that you have your neck warmers to keep you warm, it might make a terrible scenario far worse. The same is true for companies that borrow money to fund new endeavors, construct or improve buildings or plants, or cover short-term operating expenses. It won't cause trouble if you handle your debt wisely, but be careful not to accumulate more. Dark times might result in missing payments, which can raise questions about a company's creditworthiness for the future if it needs loans. Investors are also affected by these worries and may decide to move their money from debt-ridden businesses to those with more liquid assets. Berkshire should always be flush with cash, according to Buffett. He addressed a letter to shareholders in 2008, restating ideas he had previously expressed.

"However, I have promised to always have more than enough money to run Berkshire for you, the rating agencies, and myself. Never should we rely on the goodwill of others to fulfill our duties for the upcoming day. If forced to decide, I won't give up even a single night's sleep for the possibility of greater riches. It's telling that a seasoned investor like Buffett forbids Berkshire to incur a high debt load. How should the rest of us defend the need for debt if he (one of the greatest investors of all time and an unrivaled mathematical genius) doesn't believe it? It unquestionably increases your danger. When possible, avoiding it like Buffett does is the safest course of action. Buffett further reduces his risk by concentrating his investments in US-based businesses rather than purchasing overseas stocks.

Nevertheless, over the years, Berkshire has held a small number of shares in a number of foreign corporations, including the Irish brewer Guinness, the Chinese oil company PetroChina, and a few Irish banks.

Additionally, Berkshire has recently made investments in the Brazilian payments company Stoneco, new software IPO snowflake (a company for data-intensive applications without operational burden), Amazon.com, Verizon, and the Bank of New York Mellon. It also owns outright shares of BYD, a Chinese manufacturer of batteries, electric cars, and mobile phones. Buffett, though, like to invest in firms that are local. Buffett has chosen to forgo international investments partly due to the dangers they involve, despite the fact that doing so provides many benefits, such as the opportunity to invest in younger, faster-growing businesses in emerging economies. These hazards include being aware of the geopolitical context of each market, the various account restrictions, and the additional complexity it brings to investment choices. Every investment carries some risk, but where it can be avoided, there is no need to take on additional risk.

Distinguish your thoughts from the crowd.

Don't base your decision on the words or behavior of other individuals. When Buffett started managing money in 1956 with $100,000, he was dubbed an oddity. He never worked on Wall Street; instead, he worked in Omaha, and he never disclosed where he was investing the money of his partners. As a result, the majority of analysts projected that he would fail, but 14 years later, when he terminated his partnership, it was revealed that the partnership was worth more than $100 million. He thereby disproved their predictions. Benjamin Graham, Buffet's guru, frequently says, "You're not correct when other people agree with you. Only when your facts and analysis are accurate can you be right. As an investor, you must be able to think for yourself, which occasionally means being willing to stand out from the majority. Don't just heedlessly follow the throng.

When Warren Buffett decides an idea is a good one, he throws everything into it. That's unusual in the world of investing, where most individuals would take tiny investments initially and watch these stocks, or would simply make sure that a stock made up no more than 10% (or some other arbitrary amount) of their overall portfolio. Buffett is of the opinion that when such possibilities arise, you should seize them with both hands and move quickly.

Buy Just What You Can Understand.

One of the simplest ways to make a preventable error is to get involved in investments that are unnecessarily complicated. Most of us work in just a few industries for the duration of our whole lives. The majority of the publicly traded companies in these areas are outside of our direct experience, while we may have a fair understanding of how these specific marketplaces operate and know which companies are the greatest in their field. Buffett didn't imply that you couldn't invest money in these market sectors when he said, "Only buy what you understand," but you must be cautious. Can you, for instance, forecast the likelihood that a biotechnology company's medication pipeline will be successful, the upcoming key adolescent fashion trend, or the upcoming technological advancement that will have an impact on the growth of semiconductor chips? Although many of these organizations' complicated difficulties have an impact on the revenue they produce, the truth is that it is impossible to forecast them.

There are far too many opportunities to pursue rather than getting bogged down in researching a business or sector that you have no interest in. It's one of the reasons Warren Buffett has shied away from investing in the technology industry. Move on to the next concept if, after 10 minutes, you still don't have a clear understanding of how a company makes money or the key factors affecting its industry. By remaining inside your area of expertise, you can avoid many common financial blunders.

Buffett is of the opinion that thorough study must be done before purchasing stock in a firm. Knowing a ticker symbol alone won't help you much; you also need to know what the company does, how it produces money, and who is in charge. This level of recognition is an effective way to determine whether you are looking at a business with a strong moat and a long-lasting competitive advantage or just another here-today-gone-tomorrow phony. Folks, you can't learn all that without putting in the effort.

The amount of research some of us do before purchasing a new laptop, car, phone, or refrigerator is amusing, but when it comes to investing our hard-earned money in purchasing a business (also known as investing in public companies), the majority of us are content to listen to others and do as little as possible ourselves.

Fortunately, compared to Buffett's early reading and study on firms, our lives are a lot simpler today. We now have instant, largely free access to financial information thanks to the internet, which seems endless. To view corporate filings, Buffett has to go in person to the Securities and Exchange Commission. He claimed, "That was the only way to get them." The narrative for certain Moody's and Standard & Poor's reports was similar. He would have to appear and ask for the documents he needed on particular businesses from their library, then sit and read through them slowly while making notes for himself. Even a copy machine wasn't available to him. Buffett used to lug around those enormous Moody's and Standard & Poor's guides when he wasn't physically hanging out at either of those agencies or the Securities and Exchange Commission. He developed this practice while attending Columbia Business School, where he learned investing research from his mentor Ben Graham.

These are not 100-page paperbacks; rather, the hardcover Moody's manuals, which cover practically every publicly traded firm, have 10,000 pages. Buffett has claimed that when working as a stockbroker at his father's Omaha firm, he looked through each company in the 10,000-page Moody's guidebook twice. Buffett also has no problem visiting businesses in person to learn more about them and speak with management face-to-face. When he was a graduate student, he started doing this with

GEICO, a firm that is now entirely owned by Berkshire Hathaway. Buffett learned it and wanted to look into it more.

The company was well-liked by Graham's investing firm. On a Saturday, he arrived at GEICO's corporate headquarters and soon found himself questioning a vice president about the business's finances and prospects. Soon after, Buffett made a significant investment in GEICO's stock using his funds. It is rumored that he has an insatiable need for knowledge and devours whatever he can get his hands on.

He absorbs information like a sponge, far more than is physically feasible. He reads a ton of books, business publications, and annual reports. He is said to read at least five newspapers daily and has been a consistent Wall Street Journal reader since his college years. He had made arrangements to have the Wall Street Journal brought early to his office every morning while he lived and worked back in Omaha so that he could stay ahead of the curve when it came to the most recent financial news. From the moment he enters his tiny Omaha office until he leaves for home, Buffett typically spends his days reading. Every year, he reads roughly 700 annual reports, giving each one 45 minutes to read cover to cover. He has perfectly optimized this laborious procedure. He's remarked before about how uninteresting his time at the office would appear to an outsider given that he spends the most of the day just lounging about reading. His nights are usually the same.

His three adult children have spoken about how their father loved to read when they were little. After dinner, he would go to his study upstairs and read until he fell asleep, and they were aware not to disturb him unless absolutely necessary. Buffett's motivation to learn whatever he can is pure curiosity. He has gained the ability to make sophisticated financial judgments more quickly thanks to this habit than most of us would feel confident doing. He spends a lot of time studying the financials of nearly any company he would be interested in acquiring, so he can rapidly evaluate potential transactions. Buffett reads to stay prepared for new business concepts in addition to keeping up with the financials of Berkshire's current assets, as he noted when asked about this practice, "Noah did not start building the ark when it was raining." Buffett has an extraordinary capacity for information recall and a razor-sharp mind.

The author Andrew Kilpatrick stated in his book Warren Buffett: "He is a genius and the rest of us mortals can't relate to that. Although it certainly helps, you don't need to possess his remarkable intellect and near-perfect memory to succeed as an investor - remember Buffett's quote about temperament triumphing IQ in investing. If you tell people he can read and absorb a book in one sitting, people don't believe it because they can't do it. However, like him, you must have a thirst for knowledge. It's not necessary to read five newspapers a day, ask for the Wall Street Journal to be delivered early, or spend your evenings holed up at home reading annual reports. To become a great investor, though, you must enjoy businesses and improve your academic performance. For instance, you must master the fundamentals of accounting in order to comprehend a balance sheet and avoid becoming perplexed while talking about accounts receivable or goodwill.

To understand how different business models generate revenue, you must read about them. What distinguishes, for instance, the business strategy of cheap goliath Walmart from that of jewelry retailer Tiffany's? Despite the fact that they are both retailers, their business models are very dissimilar. Tiffany prefers to offer fewer, higher-quality items but makes more money off each one while Walmart decides to sell a lot of things with little markup, a high volume/low margin approach. You need to become used to the odd vocabulary of business, and the best way to do so is to embrace reading about it. It helps to have a healthy awareness of your surroundings. Buffett's insatiable curiosity is a significant advantage for him. You can never predict where your next fantastic investment concept or opportunity will come from.

You have the mental capacity to accept novel concepts when you have an open mind to learning about everything and everything. Now, this is not to say that Buffett spends a lot of time reading about and keeping up with information on businesses outside of his area of expertise (and neither should you). Due to his curiosity, it isn't hard to picture him keeping up with some businesses outside of his sphere of expertise, albeit without the same depth and fervor he devotes to those within it. It is quite improbable that Buffett spends a lot of time reading about tech businesses, save from those that he finds fascinating, like Microsoft, Google, and Apple. He might find it difficult to forecast their future cash flows because of how quickly-evolving and unpredictable the technology sector is, which could be one explanation for that. He directs his attention and mental resources elsewhere. The takeaway is clear: Unless you're certain that delving deeply into new fields will bring them within your sphere of expertise, you're probably better off continuing to learn as much as you can and expanding your understanding of the businesses and industries you are already familiar with. Buffett's capacity to avoid "confirmation bias," the very human inclination to look solely for facts that supports a judgment we have already reached rather than challenging it, is another crucial quality. News that appeals to us is what we tend to favor; news that challenges us is less common. It's the adult equivalent of shrieking nonsense while jamming your fingers in your ears to block out what someone else is saying. Negative information should never be avoided or disregarded by investors, though.

Making investing decisions with confirmation bias can make mistakes worse because it can make you reluctant to acknowledge that you made a mistake in the first place. Buffett is remarkably adept at owning up to mistakes he has made (more on making and owning up to mistakes later in this chapter).

When fresh evidence surfaces that refutes a belief he had, it may hurt his ego and anger him, but he analyzes it and accepts it. Buffett writes, "So far, I have been dead wrong. I have been mistaken about a purchase I made of the oil giant ConocoPhillips when oil prices were sky-high and then they crashed. Even if prices should rise, nevertheless, the poor timing of my acquisition has cost Berkshire many billion dollars. When you don't take the time to reflect on your assumptions, examine what can go wrong, or discover what you might be overlooking in your analysis, you immediately raise your risk. As was already mentioned, Buffett thinks you should take every precautionary

101

measure at your disposal to lower your risk. Making sure you take into account other opinions is helpful in this regard.

Nobody is perfect at it, therefore you won't be. But it's incredibly beneficial to attempt to consider all perspectives, not just those that support your position. Regarding the human propensity to seek acceptance for one's investment ideas, Buffett wrote in a 2008 letter to Berkshire Hathaway shareholders, "acceptance though is not the purpose of investing. Because it numbs the brain and makes it less open to fresh information or a reexamination of previously formed judgments, approval is frequently unproductive. Watch out for investment activity that gets cheers; the best moves are typically met with yawns.

Keep things simple and avoid making them too complicated.

Buffett thinks that investing successfully is much easier than many experts portray it to be. Buffett argued, "Why should I buy real estate when the stock market is so easy? " in response to a friend's suggestion that he try his hand at real estate.Value investing concepts appear so straightforward and commonplace, he said. To spend time in school and earn a PhD in economics seems pointless. If you have to go through too much investigation, something is wrong, said Warren Buffett in response to a question about how he and Munger conduct "due diligence" on the businesses they purchase. In 1986, Berkshire Hathaway ran a newspaper ad seeking businesses to buy, which read: "We don't use any staff and won't need to discuss your business with commercial partners." You will only communicate with me and Charles Munger, vice chairman of Berkshire.

Mark Hulbert, a Forbes columnist, did some math and found that when separating Buffett's top 15 decisions from the thousands of others, his long-term performance will be mediocre. Buffett frequently said, "All there is to investing is picking good stocks at good times and staying with them so long they remain good companies."

When there is an edge, only invest.

Every successful investor has an edge, according to one of Warren Buffett's quotes: "Defining what your game is, where you are going to have an edge is enormously important." Each investor has a distinct advantage over others due to this difference. This edge could be psychological (such as emotional resiliency or temperament), lateral thinking, intellectual (typically derived from creativity), low-cost permanent capital, or access to better knowledge in the field of investment. Additionally, it might imply a superior track record or a wider time frame than other investors. Outperformance is a combination of numerous edges, as has been demonstrated. The three things that give Buffett an advantage are reading, thinking, and emotional restraint. Buffett frequently spends more time reading and contemplating in order to limit his impulsive actions. When making investments, he is not sentimental. He is adamant that any investor who is emotional would not succeed. Buffett is also a lifelong student.

"Warren wants to identify mistaken thinking and avoid it in the future," as Charlie Munger may say.

You are paid for your errors rather than your accomplishments.

No one can be perfect at everything all the time, therefore mistakes are inevitable. What matters, however, are your strengths and areas of weakness. You can make a ton of money if you start investing early and frequently without having a significant or remarkable profession. If your initial investing attempts are unsuccessful, research and implement a fresh approach. You cannot reap the benefits of achievement unless you correctly correct your errors.

Market timing is always accurate, but typically early

This tale struck me as remarkable: Benjamin Graham, Buffett's Columbia University professor, and his father both advised him against investing in the securities industry after Buffett graduated in the 1950s. The Dow had recently reached 200 points. Back then, Buffett had $10,000. He argues that if he had waited, he would still have $10,000. In the words of Munger, "We are forecasting how people will swim against the current. I find this tale amazing because the two people who most definitely knew Buffett was a superb investor discouraged him from participating in the business because they were worried about the market conditions at the time. We are not predicting the current itself. It is challenging to concentrate on finding outstanding investors rather than making market predictions; even Benjamin Graham gave victim to the allure of making a market call.

One aspect of market timing is making future projections. However, as no one possesses a crystal ball, this technique has a high likelihood of failing. Buying stock with the intention of selling it for a profit soon after may sound perfect, but this is frequently not the case. There are always going to be people who are lucky, but luck is precisely what it is, and timing the market consistently is very hard. This implies that a person could enjoy success with one stock but lose everything with the subsequent trade. Timing the market might have unforeseen financial effects as well. Frequent trading raises brokerage commission fees when using a broker. Your broker will receive more commission the more stocks that are bought and sold. Even worse, the investor is required to pay the commission whether or whether they make a profit.

Even in investing, patience is a virtue.

"I've never swung at a ball while it was in the pitcher's glove," Buffett claimed. When opportunities present themselves, you take action. I've had both bursts of creativity and dry spells throughout my life. Next, if I have an idea, I'll act on it. Investing demands a huge amount of patience, and most individuals find it difficult to stay calm during a tumultuous period. If not, I won't do a darn thing. As a result, individuals switch their attention from long-term objectives to immediate concerns, allowing recency bias to rule their judgment. The propensity to assume that recent trends and patterns will persist is known as recency bias. Even the most knowledgeable long-term investors lost the patience and discipline necessary to stay focused during the 2008 crisis, which lasted for months. The capacity for patience is necessary for success. Along the path to success, a certain amount of discipline and courage may be necessary, but patience is the most important quality.

The key to turning discipline and commitment into progress is patience.

Never skimp on the standard of your work.

Saying "no" to complex businesses and industries is very simple, but identifying high-quality firms is far more difficult. Over the past 50 years, Warren Buffett's investment strategy has changed, now concentrating almost entirely on purchasing high-quality businesses with long-term potential for continuing growth. He held the opinion that even if a stock was purchased at a suitably low price, there will eventually be some unexpectedly positive news that would allow you to sell the position for a respectable profit. Warren's opinions on "cigar butt" investing modified as he accumulated more investing experience. He claimed that it is stupid to approach buying firms in that way unless you are a liquidator. The price that initially appears to be a steal may not actually be. In a challenging industry, as soon as one issue is resolved, another one emerges.

Additionally, the meager returns earned by these businesses significantly reduce the investment's initial worth. The return on invested capital is one of the most crucial financial statistics you can use to evaluate any business' quality. Buffett had similar ideas in mind when he developed the famous quote: "It is far better to buy a wonderful company at a fair price than a fair company at a wonderful price." Businesses that generate high returns on the capital they invest in their operations have the ability to multiply their earnings more quickly than those that do not. As a result, these businesses' inherent worth increases with time. High returns on capital build value and frequently signal an economic depression, as Warren Buffett would remark, "Time is the friend of the wonderful business, but an enemy of the mediocre." Instead of succumbing to the urge to purchase shares of a firm trading for "just" 8x earnings or a dividend stock yielding 10%, make sure you are comfortable with the business quality of the company.

Plan to hold a stock you purchase indefinitely.

When a high-quality company has been bought at a fair price, how long should it be retained, Buffett was asked. In response, he said, "Don't even consider holding a stock for ten minutes if you aren't thinking about owning it for ten years. Our preferred holding time has ended. It's obvious that Warren Buffett favors the buy-and-hold strategy. Some of his positions have been with him for many years. It is challenging to identify good companies with a continuously bright long-term future; this is why Buffett maintains a concentrated portfolio. A quality firm will also appreciate over time since it generates significant profits. Fundamental changes in a stock's price can take years to manifest, benefiting only long-term investors. Investment returns are sabotaged by frequent trading. Taxes and trading commissions limit returns when you buy and sell stocks too frequently.

The stock market is made to move money from those who are active to those who are waiting. Warren Buffet.

Diversification has its risks.

Warren Buffett owns a small number of portfolio stocks, the exact reverse of what the majority of mutual fund investors do. Buffett's highest investment was 35% of his entire wealth as of 1960. Buffett knows the market rarely offers exceptional companies to buy at fair prices, which is evidence that he invests with confidence based on his finest ideas. You'll observe that the majority of our equity holdings are substantial, Buffett stated. We make long-term investment decisions based on the same criteria we would use to decide whether to purchase 100% of a functioning company: A purchase price that is appealing when compared to the value yardstick to a private owner, competent and honest management, competent and competent long-term economic features, an industry we are familiar with, and an industry whose long-term business qualities look competent to judge. Finding investments that match these criteria is challenging, which is one of the main reasons we have concentrated holdings.

It is not possible to locate 100 securities that meet our investment criteria. However, we are perfectly content to concentrate our holdings in a far smaller amount than what we do find to be appealing. So, when, in a rare instance, a business fits these requirements, he seizes the opportunity. It makes sense why he said: "Opportunities come rarely. So instead of setting out the thimble when it starts to rain gold, put out the dollar. On the other hand, some investors overdiverse their portfolios out of fear, ignorance, or both. Owning 100 stocks makes it nearly hard for an investor to stay up to date on news that affects the firms in those stocks. A portfolio with excessive diversification also increases the likelihood of having poor companies, which lessens the impact of its high-quality assets. "Diversification is a protection against ignorance," says Warren Buffett. For those with experience, it makes very little sense.

Even better, according to Charlie Munger, "Madness is the idea of excessive diversification."

The majority of news is noise, not news, and stockholders frequently use their fellow shareholders' erratic and frequently irrational conduct to influence their own behavior. Some investors think it's vital to listen to experts and, worse still, act on their advice since there is too much talk about the markets, the economy, interest rates, and the price behavior of stocks. Warren Buffet

The 80-20 rule becomes the 99-1 rule when it comes to financial news; we should only credit 1% of the investing decisions we make to the financial news we read. The majority of news stories and TV debates aim to stir up interest and arouse feelings that will make people do almost anything. Concentrate your investment efforts on companies that have overcome every improbable obstacle imaginable. Does it matter, for instance, that Johnson & Johnson stock has dropped 10% since the first purchase or that Coca-Cola missed its quarterly earnings projections by 4%?

However much their stock prices may fluctuate as these issues develop, the answer to these concerns is remains an emphatic "no." Financial news organizations inflate these difficulties because they want to stay in business. Always consider how a news story may affect your company's potential for long-term profitability as an investor. Remember that the company in which you invested is referred to as "your company" in this situation. Do the opposite of what the market is doing if your response is no. Consider purchasing more Coca-Cola stock as an example, even though the earnings report showed a 4% decline, as the cause was transient. The stock market is extremely unpredictable and active. This excellent investment advice is to be very picky about the news you listen to and to act considerably less on it.

Although investing is not complex, there is no quick fix.

"A rocket scientist is not required. The person with a 160 IQ does not always outperform someone with a 130 IQ in the game of investing. Warren Buffet

One of the biggest misunderstandings about investing is that only experienced stock pickers can make profitable decisions. Raw intelligence, however, is one of the least reliable indicators of investment success. Following Warren Buffett's investment approach doesn't need much creativity, but continuously beating the market and avoiding bad decisions is extremely challenging for anyone. Investors must also understand that there is no such thing as a magic formula, set of rules, or "easy button" that may provide outcomes that outperform the market. It has not yet existed and will never be made.

"Investors should challenge historical models. These models, which are typically created by a nerd, may appear impressive, but investors need to understand how they work. Watch out for geeks carrying formulas. Warren Buffet

Anyone who asserts to have such methods is either foolish or a con artist. The vendors or makers won't need to sell books or subscriptions if such mechanisms are in place. While following a broad set of investment rules is acceptable, investing still involves thought, which should be done.

"Investing isn't meant to be simple. Those who find it simple are foolish. Chuck Munger

Understand the distinction between cost and value.

Despite a terrible recession looming, I never considered selling my farm or New York real estate during the enormous financial panic that occurred in late 2008. It would have been stupid for me to even consider selling it if I had owned 100% of a reliable company with promising long-term prospects. Why then would I have sold my stocks, which represented little stakes in fantastic companies? Although any one of them could eventually let people down, as a collective, they had a good chance of succeeding. – Warren Buffet

During the financial crisis, there were a lot of deals to be had because most investors were eager to liquidate all businesses without considering their viability or long-term earnings potential. During the recession, the majority of businesses continued to hone their competitive advantages, and they came out of the crisis with more promising prospects. The stock price of a corporation and its underlying business value were momentarily independent. Warren Buffett advised long-term investors to buy quality when it was on sale in order to maximize returns. Price is what you pay, as Warren Buffett would say. You get what you pay for. The future stream of cash flow for a corporation doesn't change since stock prices fluctuated due to investor sentiment. Investors must distinguish between price and value and concentrate their efforts on high-quality companies that are now trading at the most competitive pricing.

The best motions are monotonous.

"We don't try to identify the few winners that will stand out in a sea of unproven businesses. We are aware that we lack the intelligence to pull that out. Warren Buffet.

The goal of investing is not to have fun, and dividend growth investing is still a conservative approach. Investing in businesses with a track record of success is frequently preferable to looking for the next big thing in a developing sector. The objective is still to find high-quality companies whose value will continue to increase over time. Your portfolio results will take care of themselves if you do it correctly. Medicine, toothpaste, beverages, and snacks are among the basic goods and services offered by the majority of businesses with long and prosperous corporate histories. Although some sectors may not be the most interesting, their leaders are protected by their sluggish rate of change. This tendency has benefited the majority of the companies included in the dividend kings and dividend aristocrats indices.

Be cautious of investment activity that receives applause; the best decisions are typically met with yawns. Warren Buffet

You don't have to be a hero or try to impress someone with your investments; boring can be lovely.

Most investors would be comfortable with inexpensive index funds.

Buffett stated that the trustee should "put 10% of the cash in short-term government bonds and 90% in a very low-cost S&P 500 index fund (I suggest Vanguard's)" when he passes away and his Berkshire Hathaway shares are donated to charity. I think the trust would outperform most investors that employ high-fee managers in the long run, whether they be individuals, institutions, or pension funds.

Even if Warren Buffett is the greatest successful stock picker of all time, isn't it odd that he supports passive index funds?

Low-cost passive indexing should be taken into consideration by many investors as it might be a great strategy for them, especially if they aren't focused on generating consistent dividend income. Aside from that, most stock pickers are unable to support their exorbitant prices with even a passable performance.

Only take advice from people you know and trust.

No matter the level of assurances provided by management that the value-diluting action taken was a one-time event, shareholders will suffer for a long time from the price/value ratio afforded to their stock (in comparison to other stocks) once management shows more sensitivity to the interests of the owners. Warren Buffet

In all of his shareholder letters and the few interviews he has given, Buffett emphasized the value of funding management teams who are dependable and capable. That demonstrates how meticulous he is in choosing partners and management. Their activities have a long-term impact on an investment. Like many investors, you might not have the resources to thoroughly assess the morals and abilities of a CEO of a publicly traded firm for financial purposes, but you can choose who you pay attention to when selecting your assets and portfolios. Sadly, there are many con artists operating in the financial sector who seek to take advantage of investors' hopes, fears, and greed in order to profit quickly. The majority of financial "gurus" and talking heads in advertisements do so in order to profit from the trades of investors or attract new customers.

We've long believed that stock forecasts merely serve to enhance fortune-tellers' reputations. Warren Buffet

You must just consider the facts as a value investor and have reasonable expectations. No investing expert cares more about your investment portfolio than you do, so be careful who you trust.

Earnings provide equities with value.

Stocks are worth what they earn or what they promise to earn in the future. "We choose stocks that have a high return on investment when there is a good chance that they will continue to do so. For instance, Coca-Cola was selling for nearly 23 times our earnings the last time we bought it. That equals roughly five times earnings when we multiply our purchase price by the current earnings. It involves the interaction of capital used, capital returned on, and future capital generated in relation to the current purchase price. Over time, the stock will rise if the company does well.

Reduce your debt.

According to Buffett, borrowing money is like a dagger tethered to a company's steering wheel and pointed right at its heart. You'll eventually run into a pothole. Charlie Munger added his two cents: "Warren and I are hesitant to purchase stocks on margin. When you possess securities that have been pledged to others, there is always a minor danger of disaster. The ideal borrowing situation is one where nothing temporary can bother you. Additionally, Buffett claims that the U.S. trade imbalance is a rapidly growing debt backed by American assets: "Our riches are our curse in attempts to achieve a trade balance. Commercial realities would limit our trade deficit if we had less wealth. But since we are wealthy, we can continue to exchange earning properties for consumption goods. We resemble a wealthy family that sells land every year to fund a lifestyle that is not supported by its existing output. It's all joy and no pain until the plantation is gone. But ultimately, the family will have exchanged their life as owners for that of tenant farmers.

A system of giving import certificates when a particular amount of products is exported, whereby it would be essential to have a certificate to import that same worth of goods into the United States, is Buffett's suggested solution to the trade dilemma. An importer could buy or trade the exporter's certificates. The certificates would develop into a buy-sell-barter system, with imports and exports always having equal value. In a 1987 op-ed column for the Washington Post, Buffett outlined his plan. Buffett's suggestion would raise import prices and decrease American consumption of foreign goods (which would result in us consuming more than we generate), thus there wasn't a stampede to embrace it.

The Different Kinds And Uses Of Investing

Making money is the main goal of investing. When thinking about trading financial products on a stock exchange, there are many different ways to make money. Investing will always be done for financial gain. How much money can you expect to make from the investment you choose to make? The method of earning money is equally important.

Stocks can be purchased for growth, income, and discount. The most frequent sorts of investing are growth investments. There is also day trading for profit, which will be covered, however briefly.

Stocks and Growth

Always a wonderful example of growth and stock prices is Google. Google first appeared to be just another search engine firm in 2004 when it was created. In terms of search engines in general, Yahoo was the pioneer, with Microsoft vying for a piece of the action. Browsers like Crazy Browser, Mozilla Firefox, and others start to emerge as tiny search engine businesses. Additionally, there were a number of search engines like Ask.com that were made to respond to queries entered into the search field. The world of search engines today appears entirely different after 12 years. Not only does Google have the largest user base and fastest-growing market share when it comes to the number of people using Google Chrome and Google for searches globally, but it also has the most products, including Google Chromecast, Google Analytics, and AdWords.

Powerful and appearing to have grown overnight is Google. Anyone who invested during the IPO has profited significantly from their equity, including dividends. You would have needed to have thought it was more than just a standard search engine in order to profit from a stock like this. You have to have faith that it would develop into the business that it is now. Research is necessary. In addition to the necessary research, you also need to find out what other people are saying about the business and whether the anticipated future growth will actually occur.

When you buy in stocks for growth, you are well-versed in the company's industry area, the capabilities of the CEO and senior management, and the company's growth objectives. Initially, Google was a search engine. It has grown to include much more, including computers, online TV options, books, and more.

You can buy shares of a firm and anticipate long-term profit if it demonstrates that it has funds through the IPO and planned products that will sell.

Let's use oil as an illustration. You can buy commodities like oil. Since we have been using oil for so long and there are fewer and fewer places to drill, oil reserves are famously scarce. Oil stocks are rising because there is a constant imbalance between supply and demand. Oil prices fall when it is announced that oil held in reserve will be released, which lowers the cost of oil-related goods like petrol at the pump. There is a theory that oil will eventually run out totally and that there won't be any more places on earth to drill. There are also theories that oil can be found in locations that are difficult to drill or call for apparatus that is still being developed.

As long as you have faith that oil will continue to be discovered beneath the surface of the earth or of the oceans, prices will continue to fluctuate, offering opportunities for years of profit.

Let's examine tablets as yet another illustration of growth-oriented stocks. The newest gadget to hit shelves is tablets and iPads. They are the ideal replacement for large laptops because they are portable and tiny. When tablets first came out, you had to decide which firm would have the finest technology and the capacity to meet consumer demand, which led to the tech industry's continuing expansion.

In a similar vein, 3D televisions were once predicted to be the next big thing. Tablets became popular, whereas 3D televisions are largely still a thing of the 1980s. Now that curved TVs are available, most people are content with their thin, flat TVs and don't see the benefit of switching to one with a curve. However, these curved TVs are supposedly better. Would it be wise to invest in a business that entirely switches to their curved TV line? Most likely not. When you visit a store, you will notice that 80% of the customers have flat, non-curved TVs in their carts.

You need to understand the industry when investing based on corporate growth, in terms of the stock price continuing to rise owing to the stability of the firm and its R&D ideas. In order to reap the benefits of a recently launched initiative based on stock price rises, you must also be prepared to invest for the long term.

The decision then becomes whether to hold onto your shares, take the capital as well as the profit, or simply the profit. By taking only the profit, you can protect your earnings from the most recent stock price increase while still maintaining ownership of the company as it works on new projects. Stock prices might rise to an overpriced level where they eventually start to decline on their own. This is frequently the result of day traders overvaluing the stock in order to make money for the day and exiting after a few hours or eight hours.

Investing to Make Money

Choosing a growing stock that will be reliable and profitable every year is the key to making income investments. You buy the shares with the intention of living off the dividends. This option is designed so that you will always own stock in the company and pass the stocks on to the next generation so they can benefit from the dividends as well. Typically, dividends are given out every month or every three months. You should invest in a company that pays out substantial dividends, or you should buy stock in several businesses that do so. If you are successful in looking for companies with high dividend yields, you may be able to use the dividend income to finance a trip, pay your mortgage, or even lead a modest lifestyle. Not everyone will enjoy it. Knowing different industries, selecting solid companies that won't eliminate payouts during restructuring, and maintaining fairly large dividends are all necessary for investing for income utilizing dividends. Some businesses have distributed big dividends, lowered the amount as a result of a reorganization, and ultimately ran out of money to distribute dividends to tiny stockholders. You might be able to start generating income this way. It will require effort and intelligent decisions. It is not suitable for everyone because it requires effort to conduct adequate research and choose dividend-paying stocks.

Investing at a Discount

There is a distinction between normal value and discount value even though all investments are made for value. A stock is undervalued when it has a discount value. This explanation must be plausible, such as day traders who bought the stock, sold it, and caused a decline in its value. There are instances when a stock is undervalued as a result of the company's poor choices, and there is little chance for its value to recover. You must be able to distinguish between the several reasons why a stock has lost some of its original value. When you do discover these stocks, you can buy them at a discount and then sell them when they reach their true value to make a profit.

Another investing strategy that requires patience is this one. You must conduct thorough study and comprehend the reasons the stock is undervalued. If you are successful in analyzing the market, you will be able to decide what to buy and what won't appreciate in value over time. As an illustration, certain stocks are undervalued as a result of stock splits. Investors are deciding to sell and take their profit as the stock is going to split. Others stay there, agree to the split, and begin profiting from two stocks. It all depends on your understanding of the stock market, stock splits, and potential outcomes in the event that a new CEO is chosen.

Based on shareholder sentiment, CEOs or new managers may have an impact on a stock's value. A shareholder has the option to sell their stock if they do not trust the new corporate executives. The decrease of demand for a stock might cause its shares to start to decline if enough investors decide to sell it.

Mental Sleight-of-Mouth Techniques That Turn You From A Potential Winner to A Certain Loser

What sets you apart from those who frequently fall into mistakes and mental traps they are only partially aware of? There are undoubtedly many mental processes and methods to master in trading psychology. Here are a few things to watch out for if you want to distinguish yourself from other investors.

To start with, prevent analysis paralysis. You will need to ingest a lot of new information when you first begin trading. The information typically comes in a wide variety of formats, including some from your own background. You will launch your businesses in the international market with this information. Despite everything you know, your first trade may be rather frightening. Hopefully your first deal goes well and you make a lot of money. If you have bad luck, though, you'll begin to get why so many traders tend to give up or fail. This is what it means to "face loss," and your first loss can and will hurt.

Getting over the hopelessness, hurt, or disbelief that frequently knocks on your door as a trader is the trick in this situation. then precisely how do you do this? Now imagine that you've just spent a few hours or maybe weeks creating a fantastic trading plan. However, just one out of six swaps the world when you test it out. Any shrewd trader is aware that the true effectiveness of a strategy can only be determined with time and a sufficiently big sample of traders. However, a novice player could become frozen and abandon the game out of fear and doubt, which are frequent feelings, before even realizing the full potential of the strategy they worked so hard to establish. When nothing seems to be working, people can become quickly discouraged and give up before they have even fully engaged in the game.

It is best to acknowledge the randomness of the market. Understanding this aspect can help you develop a better mindset that can result in success. Working on market predictions can take up all of your time and give you a sense of control, but occasionally neither analysis nor predictions are successful. You may let go of a lot of the irritation that accumulates when you try to predict the markets by accepting that this is how the market functions. Simply said, the tension is not worth it. Prediction is excellent, but losing hope after a bad prediction is bad.

The horrible news is here. When it comes to penny stock purchases, where transactions may be so readily swayed, it only takes one trader to invalidate the study you have done. Even while it doesn't definitely mean you'll fail because of an invalidated analysis, you shouldn't put all of your faith in it. Depending on how much they obviously add to or subtract from the stock, one person can either increase or diminish the stock's value. So once more, it is advisable to let go of any emotional ties you may have to the market and avoid taking anything personally if it does not move in the manner you anticipated. Otherwise, despite your best efforts to follow your analysis, you can find your earnings drastically reduced or even lost.

Another beneficial mindset to adopt is one of blocking out the noise. What is the noise exactly? This happens when you have too much trading-related information from too many different sources, notably drowning out your own ideas, thoughts, and techniques. In essence, subscribing to publications, unsolicited emails, and feeds dispensing the newest tactics and ideas will only confuse you further. The best method to block out the noise is to conduct trading research whenever you want to and to occasionally disregard any messages you might receive. It is advisable to form your own opinion and move on as a lot of these newsletters, emails, and updates may conflict with one another because they are based on a range of various people's viewpoints. It's nice to learn from others, but if you aren't actively looking for it, being inundated with the newest advice or fashion may be quite confusing and obstruct your path.

It is simple to acknowledge that there is a risk. Anyone will do that when riding a roller coaster or eating some terrible chicken without giving the implications much thought. But it's crucial to consider your options and comprehend the cost of taking a risk. Even while you may not want to lose the money—who does?—you may claim that you are willing to assume the risk of the trades, this will only become apparent if you end up losing money. We cannot emphasize enough how crucial it is to accept the randomness of the market because this can lead to many of the potentially harmful feelings discussed before, especially if you were not fully prepared for the loss. Again, though, this will only be successful if you are willing to lose the money. If you are unable to, then you will unavoidably be emotionally invested in the outcome. Don't invest money that you can't afford to lose, therefore.

Another mental tip that might help you with penny stock trading is knowing when to take the profits. It seems simple enough, but many traders become obsessed with the idea of what might occur next. This resembles the mindset of a gambler, where many people continue to put bets despite having a few wins for the sheer pleasure of it and the potential to win more. Regardless of future possibilities that may seem great, a savvy trader knows when to exit the game to prevent further unwarranted losses. Knowing when to go will be a huge favor you do for yourself.

And finally, when it comes to stock trading, realizing and accepting your mistakes is another excellent strategy. It may sound funny, but occasionally refusing to accept defeat or blunders can seriously harm you. On the other side, when you acknowledge that you are mistaken, you also show that you are eager to grow from it. You can save a lot of time and money by coming to terms with these circumstances, which will free you up to move on.

You must have a winning mentality. What does this actually mean? It implies that you enter a state of mind when you approach the market with a positive outlook. In order to reduce the irrational expectations that many individuals have for themselves, you should totally embrace both what the market throws at you and what it is ready to offer. This entails not letting uncertainty or fear stand in the way. There is nothing wrong with accepting danger and coping with it if it materializes, but uncertainty and worry can quickly distract you from the competitive spirit you need to stand out.

The system you use, the tools you have, and the speed of your internet don't really matter when it comes to trading. It all boils down to how seriously you take your responsibility for the outcomes and how openly you accept what the market offers you. Having the perseverance and tenacity to see things through can bring you further than only receiving knowledge and facts-based instruction, even if the results aren't always favorable. You will have to acknowledge that this is as much a mental war as it is a physical one.

Maintain your mental fitness. This is a mental war as much as a battle of strategy. This aspect tends to increase success rates for those who are aware of it. This is because they are able to ride other people's emotional waves while avoiding their own. You can spot a lot of the volatility involved in penny stock marketing and spot a scam if you are aware of how average investors behave. We cannot emphasize enough how crucial the mental struggle is with penny stock marketing since it prevents you from making irrational decisions.

Always remember to think positively. Allow your eternal optimist to flourish just a little regardless of whether negative things occur. A trader's life can easily descend into pessimism. Even in a terrible trade, being able to look on the bright side can help you succeed.

The Best Ways To Invest In And Profit From The Met Averse

The merging of the physical and virtual worlds is known as the metaverse. It is the replacement for mobile internet and encompasses augmented, mixed, and virtual realities. Going inside a smaller computer will not be the focus of this iteration; instead, a fully interconnected and immersive environment will. The metaverse is where we work, practice medicine, interact with others, and more. It serves more purposes than just amusement.

By 2024, the metaverse business will generate 800 billion dollars, according to Bloomberg.

Investment Guidelines for the Metaverse Indexes

Time and stock index funds

The Roundhill Ball metaverse ETF is the only index fund I've seen that expressly targets metaverse businesses. The Roundhill ball metaverse index is the first worldwide index created to monitor the metaverse's performance. The index is made up of a tier-weighted portfolio of publicly traded, globally active firms like Nvidia, Roblox, Cloudflare, Snap, which owns Snapchat, unity3d, Facebook, and AutoDesk.

By using your preferred brokerage's "meta" search function and doing some research, you can locate this ETF.

Stocks

You can purchase stock in certain public companies that are active in the metaverse. Keep an eye on the following public firms in this industry: Unity technologies

Nvidia

Verizon and Qualcomm are both wireless tower companies.

Although there are end-user platforms available, the greatest business potential now exists in the behind-the-scenes architecture firms that offer all the infrastructure that keeps the metaverse functioning. Content companies are also included in this category. Keep a watch on how content creation in immersive environments is adapted by streaming services like Netflix, Hulu, Disney, and Amazon.

A Travis Scott concert in Fortnite last year made $20 million, which is a positive sign that consumers will shell out money for other media types in immersive settings.

Investing Your Time You may also invest your time in these businesses by spending it learning how to use the technology they are creating. This can entail becoming proficient in software development for a particular headgear or producing content for a new platform like Dress X.

This category is comparable to learning how to make web movies in 2006 or mobile apps in 2007. It puts you in a fantastic position to take advantage of those talents when the market changes.

Purchase a home in the Metaverse.

Purchasing virtual land is the best way to make money in the Metaverse. The property typically takes the shape of an NFT, and Decentraland is the largest—or at the very least—most well-known company for buying land in the Metaverse. In Decentraland, you can purchase virtual land.

Visit decentraland.org.

Everything is available in the "marketplace," so go there.

Other websites like Roblox, Axie Infinity, Illivium, and Sandbox are accessible.

Visit www.metaverse.properties to access the original virtual real estate provider.

You can see that they have a metaverse REIT by clicking on "invest." Real Estate Investment Trust, or REIT, is a company created to purchase real estate and distribute funds to stockholders. The only option to profit in this situation is to purchase it and then, ideally, sell it for more money. Additionally, you can build your own home there or rent it out for other people to use as a building site. The plan would be to purchase it, try to make some money in the interim, and then sell it for more money.

In Decentraland, MANA is required if you wish to purchase real estate. The coin or token connected to Decentraland is called MANA. SAND is the token for SandBox, AXS is the token for Axie Infinity, and ILV is the token for Illuvium.

For the Metaverse

You can purchase the token linked to a given Metaverse if you don't wish to own real estate there. Let's say you believe a metaverse would explode, but you don't want to invest in real estate there since it would be troublesome or expensive. In that instance, if the Metaverse does well over the long term, you can purchase the tokens and receive a similar upside.

Currently, there are four options to choose from: MANA, SAND, AXS, and ILV. Purchasing the coin or token linked to that Metaverse would be quite similar to purchasing shares, but instead.

The metaverse index

There is something called the metaverse index if you don't want to purchase specific coins or tokens. The various metaverse tokens are stored in the metaverse index. The graphic below displays a list of all the different tokens stored in this index.

You purchase the complete bundle of all the tokens in the index when you buy it. In exchange for your purchase of the metaverse index MVI, you receive a lesser quantity of each of these other cryptocurrencies. ILV now has the biggest allocation, followed by AXS, then MANA. This is unusual and a fantastic opportunity because if you invest in the index, you receive a wide variety of practically all of the Metaverses instead of picking just one that you think will succeed.

Developing NFTs

NFTs are anything else available for purchase and sale in the Metaverse, such as wearables, art, products, and avatars. Anything you can develop on a computer can be uploaded to the Metaverse. All you need are some basic design abilities.

www.ingramcontent.com/pod-product-compliance
Lightning Source LLC
Chambersburg PA
CBHW071648210326
41597CB00017B/2149